IT'S NOT EASY BEING ME!
Random Thoughts of the Modern Woman

IT'S NOT EASY BEING ME!
RANDOM THOUGHTS OF THE MODERN WOMAN

By Audrey Valeriani
Illustrations by Gigi

iUniverse, Inc.
New York Lincoln Shanghai

IT'S NOT EASY BEING ME!
Random Thoughts of the Modern Woman

All Rights Reserved © 2003 by Audrey Valeriani

No part of this book may be reproduced or transmitted in any form or by any means, graphic, electronic, or mechanical, including photocopying, recording, taping, or by any information storage retrieval system, without the written permission of the publisher.

iUniverse, Inc.

For information address:
iUniverse, Inc.
2021 Pine Lake Road, Suite 100
Lincoln, NE 68512
www.iuniverse.com

ISBN: 0-595-27481-1

Printed in the United States of America

To all of the women who have watched over me, inspired me, encouraged me and saved me. I thank you.

✶✶✶

We are women.
We say things to ourselves
that we wouldn't admit to anyone else.
And just when we think we have life all figured out,
when we think we're looking good and feeling good,
when we think things are finally
working out to our advantage,
something happens to awaken us
from that dream and bring us back to reality.
And so we return to that place
where we're really most comfortable,
where we bravely endure the calamities and catastrophes
that occur on a daily basis,
where we are sexy, beautiful, artistic,
loving, dedicated, determined, sensitive,
funny, extraordinary creatures.
We return to the hilarity of our everyday lives.

✶✶✶

****

And soon the fog will lift,

the eyes will open, the angels will sing

and a new woman will emerge.

ME–goddess of all that is energy and light.

****

Resurrection!

****

Are they looking?

Yup. I'll just keep walking.

That's it. Doing fine.

Look straight ahead.

Great. Now they're whistling.

Just ignore them. I hope I don't trip.

Oh no. I think I'm going the wrong way.

****

On the Catwalk

Partly Cloudy

✶✶✶

Just listen to her.

Going on and on about her date.

Who does she think she is being so picky?

I mean, at our age?

We used to ask what kind of car he drove.

Now all we want to know is if he has hair and teeth.

✶✶✶

Mate Expectations

****

I couldn't just take the bus.

No, I had to be a big shot

and take a taxi to the meeting.

I mean, the space shuttle goes slower than this thing.

Oh no. I think I'm gonna throw up.

****

IT'S NOT EASY BEING ME! Random Thoughts of the Modern Woman 11

On the Fast Track

Clearly, a Professional

***████

Well look at him.

This is what I get for agreeing to a blind date.

I'm gonna kill my cousin.

She must really think I'm desperate.

Black pants, white socks, greasy hair…

Oh, no way.

***████

Prince not-so-Charming

✶✶✶

Wow. Thank goodness I broke down here.

There's the mechanic over there.

Why is he looking at me like that?

Oh, I get it. Ready to take advantage of

the poor, helpless woman.

Should I tell him I'm an Assistant District Attorney?

Nah.

✶✶✶

IT'S NOT EASY BEING ME! Random Thoughts of the Modern Woman

Miss Conception

Life's wicked little pleasures

✶✶✶

I knew it. I knew it.

This is so embarrassing.

That saleswoman was so full of bull…no other dress like it.

I should have known she was lying when she

told me I looked like Heather Locklear.

✶✶✶

IT'S NOT EASY BEING ME! Random Thoughts of the Modern Woman

Cost Conscious Consequences

What are you looking at?

****

Oh I'm so exhausted, but I've got to keep going.

Just ten more pounds and I'll knock his socks off.

I've gotta be strong. Oh, I'm so tired.

What is it they say?

No pain, no…

Oh, shut up.

****

Stairway to Kevin

✳✳✳

All I need is twenty-five cents more.

Just twenty-five lousy cents!

This always happens right before payday.

Wait…here's a quarter.

No, that's a…

Oooh, I don't know what that is.

Come on, come on, please…

✳✳✳

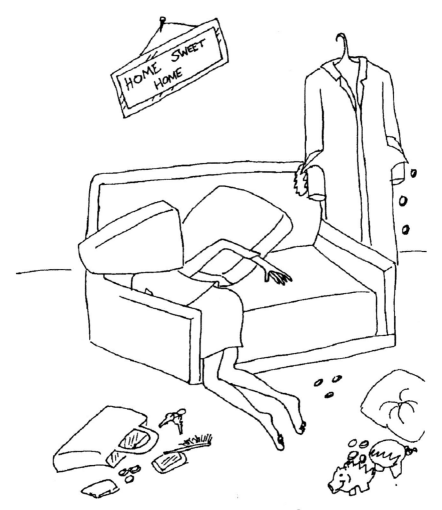

The day before payday

Really. It's you!

****

I just had to eat that last

piece of cheesecake, didn't I?

I couldn't leave the chips alone either.

And the cookies and the eggnog.

They can now spot my butt from space!

Oh, no. What have I done?

****

The Party's Over

✸✸✸

I'm so glad I cut my hair.

Hmmm…and I love this shade of lipstick.

This dress really makes me look thin too.

Wow, I'm lookin' good today.

✸✸✸

An unwelcome accessory

✶✶✶

Looks like it's just you and me, kitty.

And, of course, all that's on TV are love stories

with beautiful people and perfect endings.

Oh well, I guess it's not so bad.

I've got popcorn, ice cream

and Fluffy. Who needs a man?

✶✶✶

My furry Valentine

✶✶

There's no price on that? Fabulous.

She's looking…please, please find it.

Oh, no. She's holding it up.

Everyone's looking at me.

She's gonna call for a price check.

Announcing…

✶✶

Kill me now

A Natural Beauty

✱✱✱

Oh joy.

This has to be my favorite place in the whole world.

Sitting here, in this freezing room,

on this metal table, in a paper dress.

And what is he smiling at?

I mean, what kind of person does this for a living?

✱✱✱

Cervix with a Smile

****

Life is too short to hurry through each day

without cherishing the people we l o v e

or noticing the beauty around us.

Make it a point to…

b r e a t h e the air today,

smile at everyone and

count your blessings!

Remember…

don't take yourself too seriously,

know that you are not alone, and

keep (or get!) a sense of humor.

****

You will also enjoy

SIMPLE WAYS TO A WOMAN'S HEART:

Movie Star Maneuvers That Will Take Her Breath Away!

By Audrey Valeriani

Illustrations by Gigi

0-595-27481-1

Printed in the United States
1164300001B/75